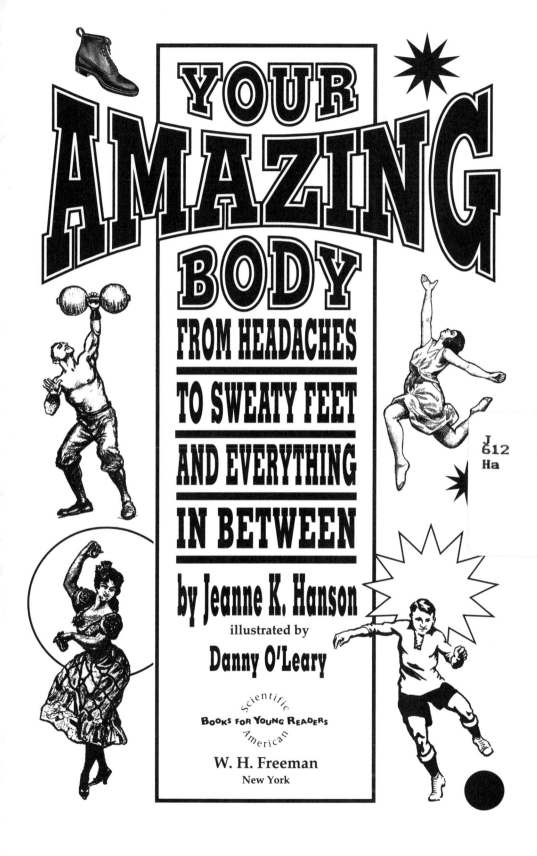

YOUR AMAZING BODY

FROM HEADACHES TO SWEATY FEET AND EVERYTHING IN BETWEEN

by Jeanne K. Hanson

illustrated by

Danny O'Leary

Scientific American

BOOKS FOR YOUNG READERS

W. H. Freeman
New York

Book design by Marsha Cohen/Parallelogram Graphics

Scientific American Books for Young Readers is an imprint of W. H. Freeman and Company, 41 Madison Avenue, New York, NY 10010.

Library of Congress Cataloging-in-Publication Data

Your amazing body: from headaches to sweaty feet and everything in between / by Jeanne K. Hanson; illustrated by Danny O'Leary.
Includes bibliographical references and glossary.
ISBN 0-7167-6533-0 —
ISBN 0-7167-6552-7 (pbk.)
1. Body, Human—Juvenile literature. [Body, Human.]
I. O'Leary, Danny, ill. II. Title.
QP37.H33 1994   612—dc20   94-17994   CIP   AC

Printed in the United States of America.
10 9 8 7 6 5 4 3 2 1

CONTENTS

TO ALL BODY OWNERS

How long would your **hair** grow if you never got a haircut? Why does a **bruise** change colors? How fast does a **sneeze** travel? If you've wondered about questions like these, this book will give you the answers. And if you haven't wondered about them, this book is a good way to begin doing so.

This exploration of your body starts with *b* for **"Bad Breath"**; goes through such body activities as **coughing, goosebumps, itching, and spitting;** and ends with *y* for **"Yawning."** You can read straight through or skip around, whichever you prefer. Laugh and learn your way through the alphabet as you find out about something pretty amazing—you!

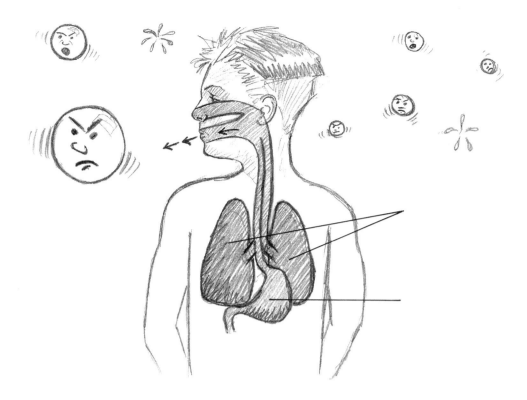

Halitosis may sound funny, but it is just another word for "bad breath"—and that's not funny! The way you get it shows something about how your body works.

After you eat, the food is broken down into tiny, tiny pieces. That way, the food can enter your bloodstream and travel to all parts of your body. Included in those parts are your lungs, which have many tiny air sacs. When you breathe out, some of the food smell comes up and out with the air you exhale. Some of the smell lands in your mouth on its way out.

Now, if you eat ice cream or bread or some other non-smelly food, there is no problem. Most foods don't stink. But if you eat garlic, onions, stinky cheese, and things like that, the smells are strong. And so, temporarily, is your breath!

You can have halitosis for a longer time if you aren't eating enough food at all, if you can't digest milk well, or if you have an illness. And sometimes the cause might be close by: Food stuck in your teeth or in your throat can stink too!

Brushing and flossing your teeth, using a mouthwash, or taking a breath mint are ways you can battle bad breath when the cause is food. If those don't help, it might be a sign that illness is causing your bad breath, and you need to have a doctor check it out.

Your eyes are exposed to wind, dirt, and particles in the air, everything from onion fumes to tiny bits of dog and cat hair. Your eyes would be damaged in less than a day if you didn't blink.

To blink you don't even have to think. When you blink, your eyes get fast little baths. Your eyelids act like windshield wipers for your eyes—complete with windshield washer fluid. The liquid that flows over your eyes when you blink is made up of water, a little salt, and a substance that fights off disease-causing bacteria. This healthful "brew" flows from nearly 30 tiny glands located along the edges of your eyelids.

Each blink uses only a little bit of this cleaning fluid. But in one day you blink out enough of it to cover the bottom of a soft-drink can.

Blinking takes less than a tenth of a second. Your eyelids flutter down, then spring back up. You do this every 6–10 seconds. In your life, you will blink about 200–300 million times!

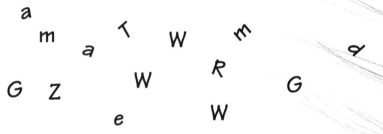

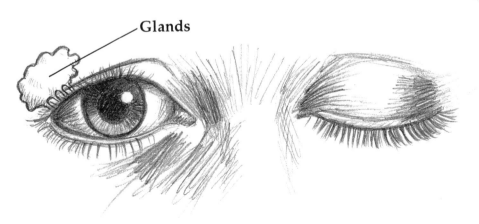

Glands

8

BLINKING

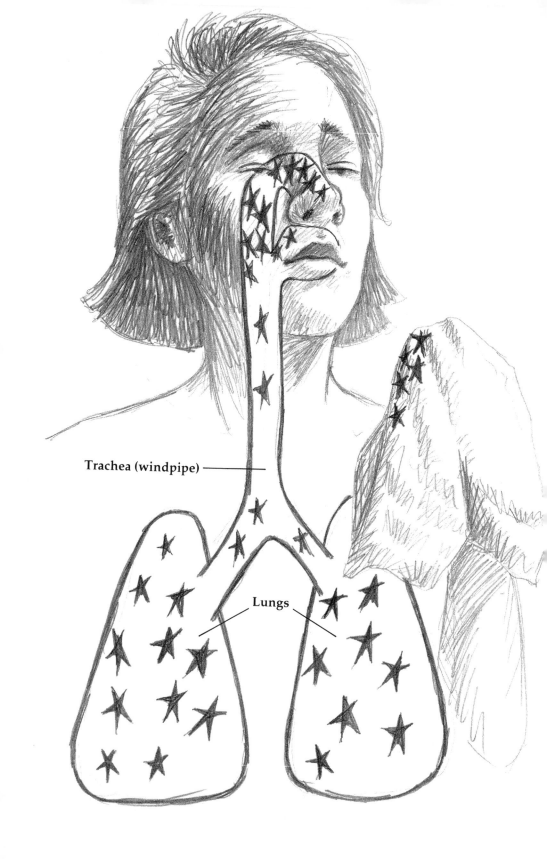

Trachea (windpipe)

Lungs

BLOWING YOUR NOSE

Snort! When the inside of your nose is irritated, you feel like blowing it. This happens when virus particles—from the virus that gave you the cold—or slimy mucus (phlegm) makes your nose feel stuffy. It also happens after you sneeze, cry, or have an allergic reaction.

Let's start with the simple snort. When you have a cold, a virus has invaded your nose, mouth, throat, and your whole respiratory (breathing) system. Although you can't see virus particles, they are living in your nose, making it irritated! No wonder you want to get them out!

By the end of the cold, your body has fought off the virus. But dead virus particles remain in your nose, mostly stuck in the mucus. It's good to get these ones out too!

When you sneeze, cry, or have an allergic reaction, water and mucus flow in your nose. This makes you want to blow too. To get rid of all the mucus, it's better to blow it out than to sniff it deeper into your nose or into your throat or lungs.

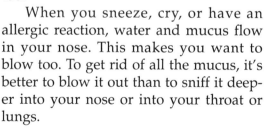

This has probably happened to you: You suddenly feel embarrassed, surprised, ashamed, afraid, angry, anxious, or eager to impress someone. If you could see your face in a mirror, it would look reddish and hot. You are blushing.

Blushing is just the nervous system of your body (which includes your nerves, brain, spinal cord, and everything connected to them) reacting to this stress. What happens is that a small part of your brain called your hypothalamus takes over. It sends a message that makes extra blood surge into your face. It also sends a message to cut off the circulation of your blood there, just for a second. These "orders" make the blood collect in the tiny blood vessels of your face—and since blood is red, your face turns reddish. Then everything quickly goes back to normal, and the blush fades.

Some people seem to blush more than others. For example, very young children almost never blush. If somebody says something like "Oh, how cute—you're blushing," you may gradually blush more often. This makes scientists think that blushing is not just automatic but also something you learn to do.

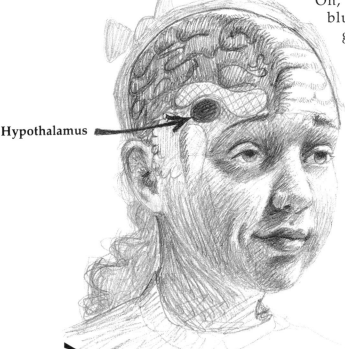

Hypothalamus

BLUSHING

13

Everybody smells bad sometimes, although nobody likes to admit to having body odor. More than a hundred different chemicals perfume your sweat, not all of them stinky. The stinkiest one—3-methyl-2-hexanoic acid—is caused by bacteria (tiny living cells) that make their home right in your armpits. These bacteria eat the chemicals coming out in your sweat. The bacteria's waste products are what makes the yucky smell.

The more sweat glands you have under your arms, the more likely you are to sweat. And the more bacteria you have living there, the worse the odor. You can see why it's good to take baths and showers!

Even when you keep clean, you still have a natural smell all your own. This is a very mild smell to humans—enough for a bloodhound to track you but not enough to drive your friends away!

How full can your stomach get? Your stomach can hold three cups of food at a time. This includes partly digested items from as long ago as four or five hours!

Sometimes you gulp air when you eat. And if you drink soda pop—which contains a gas called carbon dioxide—lots of gas enters your stomach. In addition to the gases in air and soda pop, your stomach makes more gas every day as part of its work of digesting your food.

What happens when there's no room left for all the gas? Some of it will come back up in a burp.

More formal words for burp are *belch* and *eructate*. When you burp—belch—eructate, some of what comes up, especially a gas called hydrogen, is flammable. Yes, it could cause a fire if there were lots more of it.

Burping

"Butterflies" in Your Stomach

Are you getting ready to go onstage for Act One? Have you been called on in math class, in your new school, by a new teacher? If so, you may be feeling "butterflies" in your stomach, fluttery feelings that go with nervousness.

When you are anxious like this, a chemical called adrenaline is released into the bloodstream. Adrenaline makes you want to fight or run away. This body reaction to stress has a good purpose. It shuts down part of the blood flow to places such as your stomach. Then all the energy can go to your muscles to help you fight or run away.

The only problem is that you can't battle the math teacher or run away from the stage. So you're left with a little twirl of chemicals that feels like a flutter-by of butterflies!

Choking

At the back of the throat are two very different openings. One leads down your trachea (windpipe). It is the one for breathing air and is connected to your nose too. The other one leads through the opening of the esophagus down to your stomach. That is the one you use for swallowing.

Sometimes when you are startled or distracted, you breathe in a bit of saliva (spit) that you were supposed to swallow. Or maybe a piece of meat or hard vegetable gets caught over the opening of your windpipe because you didn't chew up your food well enough. The saliva or the food blocks the airway opening. Once in a while you may vomit and some of that yucky stuff might also get caught in your windpipe. You choke—air can't get into your windpipe.

Whatever is blocking your windpipe usually comes out—in a blast of air. But, please, chew up your food!

COUGHING

A cough is a special type of breath that gets something irritating out of your breathing system. During your life, you will probably breathe in about 75 million gallons (280 million liters) of air, using about 600 million breaths to do it. Some of them will surely be coughs.

Coughing is annoying, but it is actually good for you. The most common cough comes from a cold. Sometimes coughing comes from bronchitis or other illnesses. In each case, it clears mucus (slimy, protective phlegm) from your throat, your bronchial tubes (small passageways in your throat and lungs that help you breathe), and your lungs.

In a cough the lungs are the boss. The powerful muscles around the lungs contract, then expand, pushing out air and mucus with it. As the air and mucus reach the vocal cords, on the way out, the cords partly close, allowing this "wind storm" to leave your body easily. It's a major storm. You cough at about 300 miles (nearly 500 kilometers) per hour—much faster than a hurricane!

If you're coughing all night and really can't sleep, you might consider cough syrup. There will probably be plenty of time for coughing tomorrow.

CRYING

You cry when you are sad, angry and frustrated, excited, in awe, ashamed or embarrassed, tired, even happy! Those are a lot of times. You also cry when you get something in your eye or chop up an onion. In each case the brain sends a message to your tear glands to start the tears flowing.

The tears that come from a strong feeling are chemically different from the ones that come from something irritating your eye. Emotional tears have chemicals in them caused by stress and pain. Some of these actually leave your body in the water of your tears. They are not in the "onion-type" tears at all.

All tears are made of water, salt, oil, and mucus. They each have a bit of thickener, too, to keep the tears from dripping down your cheeks before they have given your eyes a bath. In addition to the tears from emotions and

26

from eye irritations, you "cry" a bit all day and all night long, to keep your eyes from drying out. These tears just flow down your nose and throat without your even thinking about them!

When you cry, the tears flow out of two main tear glands—the lacrimal glands—on the underside of your eyelids. Sixty other tiny glands help you to cry too.

Babies don't cry tears until they are more than two weeks old, though they can tighten their faces and holler from the time they are born. There are a few people who can never cry because their body doesn't produce tears normally. If you can cry, go ahead and do it when you need to. It's good for you.

Does it snow on your sweater, even in springtime? Do you avoid wearing solid dark colors because you know you'll have white "flakes" on them soon? If so, you have dandruff!

Actually, everybody has some dandruff. Your head is a forest of hairs, with plenty of tiny skin cells in between and over their edges. And you have 19 million skin cells on every square inch of your body, including your scalp. Some of that is bound to shed!

In fact, scientists estimate that you will drop 105 pounds (48 kilograms) of skin—all in tiny flakes—from your body during your lifetime! About 10 or 11 pounds (4.5 or 5 kilograms) of this dead skin will fall off your head—as dandruff! Your skin is constantly renewing itself, so you won't lose all that weight!

Some people have more dandruff than others. That's because their scalp is drier. Among the reasons for this are too much bacteria and oil glands that aren't working properly. But no matter how much or how little you have, you can lessen the amount by shampooing regularly and sending those dead skin flakes down the drain. You don't need to use dandruff shampoo either, unless you have a special problem.

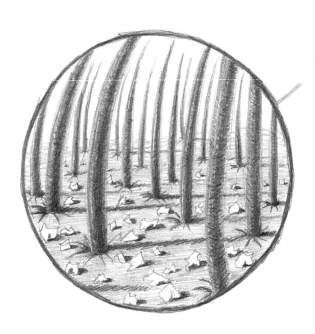

DANDRUFF

DAYDREAMING

Scientists estimate that people spend more than five hours a day daydreaming! Not all at once, of course. You may daydream for a second, a few seconds, or as much as a minute or two at a time. And you usually daydream while doing something else, like walking, getting out a book, having a snack, or brushing your teeth. After all, you have about 10 billion brain cells, enough to let you do two things at once!

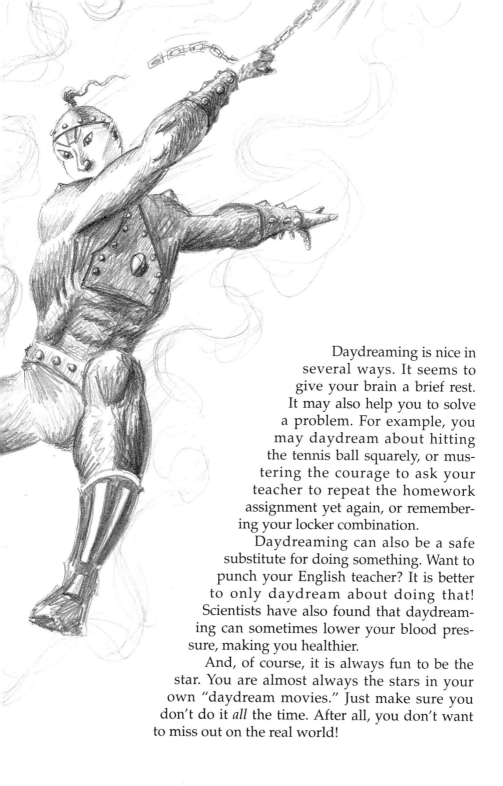

Daydreaming is nice in several ways. It seems to give your brain a brief rest. It may also help you to solve a problem. For example, you may daydream about hitting the tennis ball squarely, or mustering the courage to ask your teacher to repeat the homework assignment yet again, or remembering your locker combination.

Daydreaming can also be a safe substitute for doing something. Want to punch your English teacher? It is better to only daydream about doing that! Scientists have also found that daydreaming can sometimes lower your blood pressure, making you healthier.

And, of course, it is always fun to be the star. You are almost always the stars in your own "daydream movies." Just make sure you don't do it *all* the time. After all, you don't want to miss out on the real world!

DIZZINESS

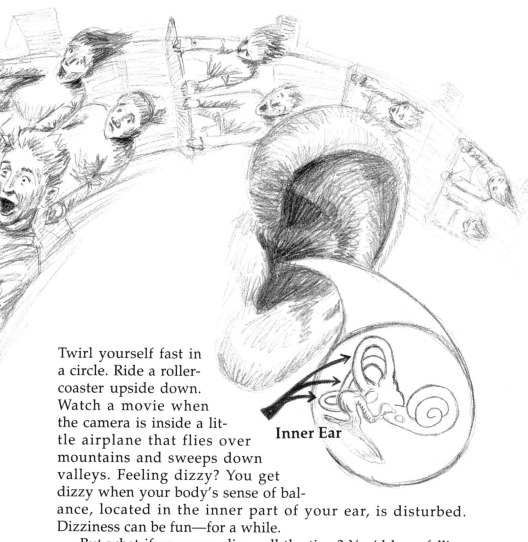

Inner Ear

Twirl yourself fast in a circle. Ride a roller-coaster upside down. Watch a movie when the camera is inside a little airplane that flies over mountains and sweeps down valleys. Feeling dizzy? You get dizzy when your body's sense of balance, located in the inner part of your ear, is disturbed. Dizziness can be fun—for a while.

But what if you were dizzy all the time? You'd keep falling down and probably couldn't eat very well. You'd actually be in danger—maybe you'd fall off a cliff or let a car smash into you as you stumbled into the street!

So your body has a way of "fixing the dizzies." Three tiny canals—filled with liquid and closed on top—are buried deep in your inner ear. They sense dizziness when the little bit of fluid in them sloshes back and forth. Then they send a message to your brain that tells you to stop doing what you're doing. You can fall down in a heap—and laugh until your dizziness goes away.

33

DREAMING

Why do you dream? There are more ideas on this than there are nights in the week! Some people think dreams are a window into your soul, showing what you fear or what you hope for—or both. Others say that dreaming is there just to clear your brain chemically at night. Still others think dreaming gives you a chance to solve a problem, be creative, store daytime memories or learning, or even feel important. Are dreams orders from another world? Or a way to foretell the future? Or are they merely a way to go safely crazy for a little while every night?

Dreams can indeed be quite crazy, and that's nothing to worry about. Everyone has anxious, angry, and sad dreams—about three or four times as many as they do happy dreams. And dreams can mix up times, places, and people, almost like a collage from art class.

If you think you don't dream, you're wrong. You're just a deep sleeper and don't remember your dreams. Everybody dreams at least one and a half to two hours at night. You dream several times throughout your night's sleep, in the periods called REM sleep—rapid eye movement sleep.

During this time you are not a blob in the bed. Your eyes dart back and forth behind your eyelids, your heart pounds, you breathe quickly, and your brain is very active.

When you think about it, dreaming is pretty strange in several other ways. You forget your dreams unless you tell someone about them right away. This is good—if your dreams were stored in your long-term memory along with what happened to you in daytime, you would quickly get confused. You'd think there really was a wolf under your bed! You also don't act out your dreams. Instead, your brain makes you temporarily paralyzed during sleep so that you don't get up and do the things you're dreaming about, like jumping out the window or dancing with the cat. This system is not quite perfect, though. Have you ever, just once, jumped out of your bed while dreaming about getting away from a bear?

Ear Popping

You are in an airplane taking off. The inner and middle parts of your ear are filled with ground-level air. As you go higher, the air pressure is lower—there is less air pushing down on things than at ground level. This new air moves into the outer part of your ear. It pushes against the membrane (lining) of your eardrum, until you feel a tiny bit of pain there.

At that point, your body decides it is time to make the two air pressures equal. Without even thinking about it, you swallow or yawn. This opens up your eustachian tubes, tiny passageways that connect your ears to your inner throat. In goes the new air and mixes with the old air to make the pressures equal. Pop goes the eardrum, as it snaps back into place. Sometimes just one pop is enough. Other times, it is a volley of tiny pops, like popcorn in a pan.

Some people's ears pop more often when they are in an airplane that's landing. The pain can get really bad, especially if you have a cold and your ears are stuffed up.

Eliminating Wastes

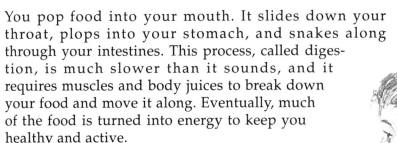

You pop food into your mouth. It slides down your throat, plops into your stomach, and snakes along through your intestines. This process, called digestion, is much slower than it sounds, and it requires muscles and body juices to break down your food and move it along. Eventually, much of the food is turned into energy to keep you healthy and active.

But some of the food becomes waste. Each day, you must get rid of more than a quart (liter) of water waste—urine— which is left over from what your body has used. And about 15 hours after you eat solid food, the part of it that was never used at all comes out as solid waste—feces. If you didn't get rid of this stuff, you'd eventually explode!

You can store nearly two cups (half a liter) of urine before you have to run to the bathroom. Your kidneys filter these liquid wastes out of your food for you. If you are under stress or just cold, the kidneys will work even harder to make

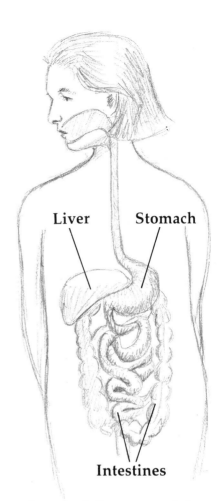

Liver   Stomach

Intestines

more urine. And they move into action fast after every meal.

The urine then moves to your bladder, where it is stored until bathroom time. When you are ready to urinate, two valves open and out it comes.

Your solid wastes are assembled gradually, as food moves more than 20 feet (6 meters) through your intestines. All along the way, the nutrients from what you ate are gradually absorbed by your body—and the wastes pushed farther down. Everything moves along at about an inch (2.5 centimeters) per minute. Then out!

When you feel troubled, hurt, disappointed, or near tears, you frown. Sometimes you even frown when you squint or concentrate. Your face has 80 muscles. One of them—the corrugator muscle—is in charge not only of frowning but of all unhappy expressions including growling and glaring. To make a frown, this corrugator muscle pushes your eyebrows down, moves them a bit closer together, and even squeezes your eyeballs a little.

Frowning has been studied by scientists who wanted to understand the relationship between emotions and facial expressions. In an experiment, actors were told to "make faces" without being told the names of the facial expressions. For example, they were told, "Furrow your brow and press your lips together slightly," instead of "Frown."

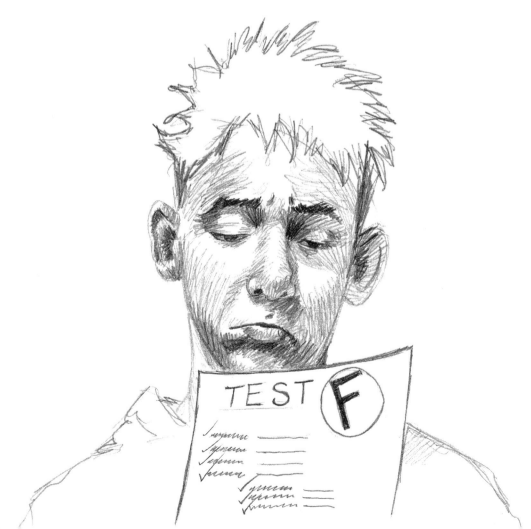

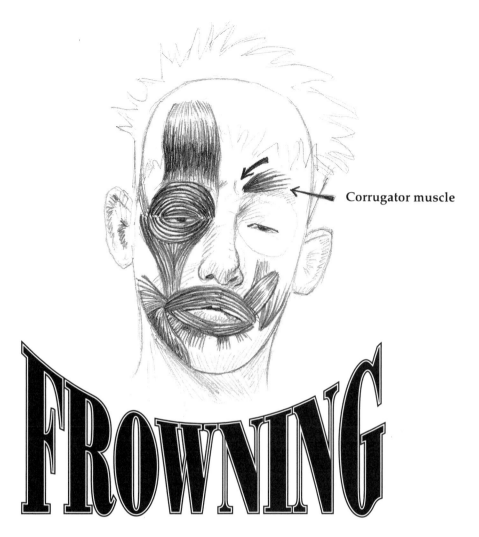

Corrugator muscle

FROWNING

As the actors were beginning to frown but before they realized what they were doing, the scientists quickly measured the actors' heart rates and skin temperatures. The actors were asked, "What are you feeling?"

The results were surprising. The body measurements turned out to be the same as those taken later on frowning people who were really feeling the emotions that naturally go with a frown. Perhaps even stranger, the actors started to feel the emotions they had put on their faces. It is as though a frown can make you upset, not the other way around. Try frowning for a minute or so, and you'll start to feel upset. Better yet, try smiling instead.

"FUNNY BONE"

It's not so funny when you hit your elbow. The tingling, shooting, piercing feeling runs all the way down your arm. You are not amused!

This unfunny feeling comes from the ulnar nerve, a long nerve that runs from the spinal cord in your back all the way down to your fingertips, on both sides of your body. It passes between the bones of your elbow. In that one area, it is not protected by muscle or fat. Your elbow sticks out, too, easy to hit. When you do hit your elbow sharply, the ulnar nerve hits against the bone or is pinched. Nerves are the messengers of pain between the brain and the rest of your body. This messenger has just been smashed. Ouch!

You have another "funny bone": your ankle bone. It sticks out, too, and it has unprotected nerves. But you don't hit it nearly as often as you do your elbow.

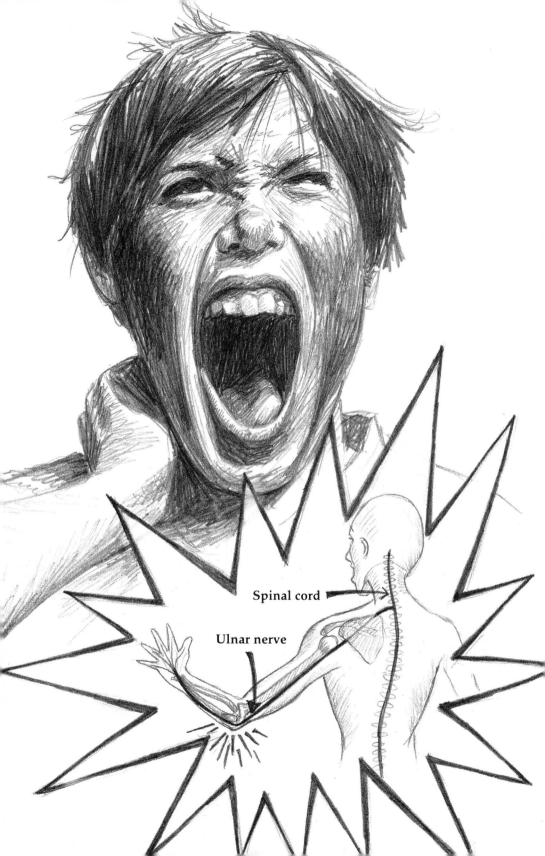

Spinal cord

Ulnar nerve

GAS

is like a burp, not from the mouth but from the other end! The formal word is *flatulence*.

The average "explosion" you create is composed of these gases: nitrogen (about 59 percent), hydrogen (about 21 percent), carbon dioxide (9 percent), methane (7 percent), oxygen (4 percent), and perhaps a little bit of hydrogen sulfide (the gas that smells like rotten eggs).

Take a look again at that list. Every time you create one of these small volleys and let out carbon dioxide and methane, you are contributing to global warming. Yes!

All these gases are created in the digestive system by your very own personal bacteria (tiny living things) that stay down there. This usually happens when the bacteria cannot completely digest something that you have eaten—often beans, vegetables, and fruit and sometimes dairy products. All of them are good for you, of course. But foods like these include some carbohydrates that just cannot be digested well by human beings.

As the bacteria in your digestive system make chemical reactions, the undigested carbohydrates release gas. Everybody else, watch out!

GAS

"Going to Sleep" in Your Hands and Feet

Have you ever sat on your foot for a long time or leaned too long on your bent hand? After a while your foot or hand felt odd. It felt dead, floppy, as though it belonged to somebody else. Then you shook it, flexed it, wiggled it around. It started to feel prickly; then it "woke up." Why?

Hands and feet "go to sleep" when you accidentally cut off part of the circulation (movement) of your blood into them. When you sit on your foot wrong or lean on your hand, the blood vessels there get narrower. Blood can't flow in and out very well. The nerves get a little squashed in your foot or hand and don't get any sensations either. For this reason, that body part feels "asleep."

When you "wake up" your foot or hand by moving it around, your nerves begin to send messages again. The message is something like "Yes, I'm down here after all." Soon the blood starts to flow more freely. The added messages and blood flow feel prickly.

GOOSEBUMPS

Goosebumps get their name from the way a plucked goose looks! You look this way too when you feel cold, frightened, or thrilled, even sometimes from other strong emotions. Just examine your arms!

Goosebumps appear when tiny muscles pull on the small tubes near your skin's surface called hair follicles. Each of these follicles holds just one hair—on your arms or elsewhere. If you had really hairy arms like monkeys do, you could *see* all your hair standing on end when you got goosebumps!

Hair is the clue to why you get goosebumps. These little bumps are probably features passed down from the ancestors that humans share with monkeys, chimpanzees, and other primates—higher apes.

Goosebumps were perfect for fluffing out body hair to fight the cold. They also made the creatures look bigger and fiercer, ready to take action.

If you never had a haircut in your whole life, your hair would grow about 26 feet (8 meters) long by the end of your life, about as long as a big classroom!

Hair grows out of tiny tubes near your skin's surface called hair follicles. About 100,000 of them are hidden under the skin of your scalp alone. Each follicle pushes out one hair. These little hair factories are especially busy in late morning and late afternoon each day, also in spring and summer. So that's when you grow the most hair.

When you see some hair caught in your comb or brush, don't worry! Most people lose 50–100 hairs every day. This happens when some of the follicle factories take a turn resting—and don't hold on hard enough to that hair. Most of this hair is replaced. But some people reach a point in their life when the hairs aren't replaced. They start to go bald.

Humans, like all other mammals, have hair. But if you lined up all the world's creatures, you'd see that many more had feathers and scales than hair as a body covering.

Hair Growing

HEADACHES

You can get a headache in too many ways! Some people get one from eating chocolate, cheese, dried fish, wheat, corn, eggs, peanuts, soda pop, or ripe bananas! Or from salt or food preservatives! You can get one from being hungry and from allergies, colds, or flu. You can also get a headache from feeling tense, from sitting too long without moving a muscle, from bad posture, from sleeping too little or even too much, from eyestrain, too much sun, and from loud noise. It's a wonder you don't have a headache all the time!

How do these things actually cause a headache? There are no exact answers. But we know they have something to do with nerves, because nerves are messengers of pain between the brain and the rest of the body.

There are four main ideas about what is happening in your head during a headache. Most scientists think that the blood vessels in your scalp first contract and then stretch more. When they stretch out, they press hard against other parts of your scalp—and that makes the pain. A second theory is that muscles in your neck and head tighten and then go into spasms (violent muscle contractions). A third explanation, which works more for people with lots and lots of headaches, is that the amounts of brain chemicals are slightly wrong. And the last theory of headaches is that extra electricity in the brain changes the supply of air up there and makes pain.

Maybe *all* these theories are right! Maybe people's heads (and brains) are too complicated for our own good!

HICCUPS

"Whup. . . whup. . . whup." You've got the hic-coughs. (That's the real way to spell "hiccups.")

A hiccough is like an "air vomit," and it works this way: Your diaphragm (the muscles above your waist area) tightens. That draws a little bit of air into your lungs. Your vocal cords snap shut to cut off the air. That turns the air into a small pocket of noise, a hiccough.

Ordinarily, the process repeats itself over and over again for a few minutes. Maybe in the middle of lunch, your book report, or your turn at the blackboard!

Why do you have this little body hobby some-times? Your stomach may have a little bit of some-thing irritating it, not enough for a major burp. Or your throat may have a little irritation. Or the two nerves that control your diaphragm—the phrenic nerves—might be out of coordination. None of this is serious.

The people you read about in the *Guinness Book of World Records* or see on TV—the ones who are hiccoughing for years like the man who had been going "whup" since 1922—probably have severe problems with their phrenic nerves. Fortunately, this is very rare!

There are a lot of stories about people gagging, gargling, giggling, and much more to get rid of the hiccoughs. A lot of this is a joke! So what should you do to get rid of the hiccoughs? Sip water slow-ly? Tug on your tongue? Have someone scare you? You don't have to pick among tricks like these—all of them work. The "cures" work because they dis-tract you from your hiccoughs. Of course, they were going to go away soon anyway.

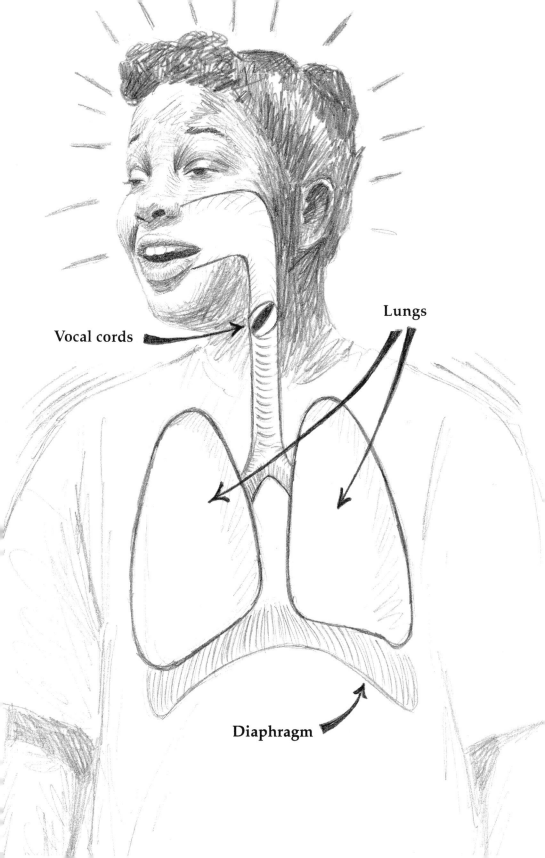

Vocal cords

Lungs

Diaphragm

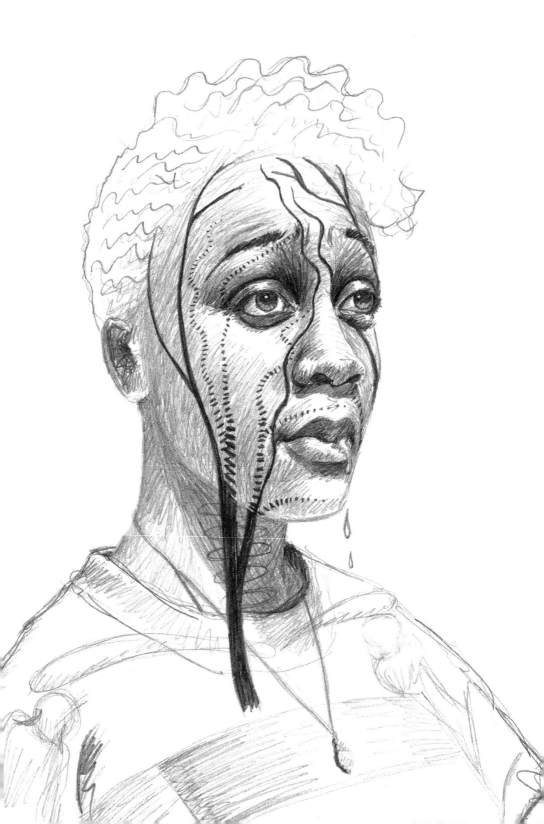

ICE-CREAM HEADACHES

Have you ever gulped an elephant-sized mouthful of ice cream? Slurped down chunks of popsicle or slushy ice in a hurry? If so, you might have gotten an ice-cream headache—short, sharp, awful pain in your forehead!

This pain comes courtesy of your two large carotid arteries. They are the ones that run along both sides of your neck, where you can feel your pulse strongly.

The carotids are the major arteries that carry blood to your brain. They have many smaller blood vessels connected to them. Some of these smaller blood vessels are just under the skin in your mouth and throat. When they feel cold, they send a message to the carotids that goes like this: "Cold here! We need to get back to a normal temperature!"

The carotids respond by sending more warm blood fast. To do this, the blood vessels all over your head have to expand to carry that extra blood. When they expand, they press against everything else in your forehead. And that's what hurts!

An ice-cream headache is over fast. After all, it doesn't take that much time for your mouth to warm up again. Now it's time to eat more ice cream, but not as fast.

57

itching itching itching itching itching itching itching itching itching

Everybody itches—you itch and scratch a little bit every day. You do it much more often, of course, if you have poison ivy, dry skin, an insect bite, athlete's foot, or another skin irritation.

There are actually two kinds of itches. One comes from your ordinary senses, and the other kind comes from allergies.

The first kind usually happens when something is rubbing against you or irritating your skin in some small way. It could be a wool hat or a tree branch or even an air current. This puts your skin on alert, as though the nerves there were saying to the brain, "Pay attention! Something is happening out here." The brain sends a message back that tells you to scratch until whatever it is goes away.

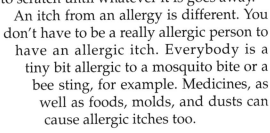

An itch from an allergy is different. You don't have to be a really allergic person to have an allergic itch. Everybody is a tiny bit allergic to a mosquito bite or a bee sting, for example. Medicines, as well as foods, molds, and dusts can cause allergic itches too.

In this kind of itch,
your body senses some-
thing foreign and releases
a substance called hista-
mine under the skin. This
is what makes your skin reddish or—if more histamine is
present—gives you a rash. When
you scratch this kind of itch, you
spread the histamine and make it
worse.

Itches may be annoying, but
they are the price you pay for
having your skin be such a good
watchdog.

LAUGHING

Giggle. Guffaw. Snicker. Whoop. Chuckle.
Howl. Chortle. Hoot. Cackle. Go ahead and
BELLY LAUGH!

Laughing is good for you. In fact, it is a little like
exercise. First, a muscle in your face called the zygomatic
muscle contracts. This makes blood become congested
(collect a lot) in your head, which boosts your blood
pressure—the pushing of blood against the artery
walls—a bit. In a hard laugh, this extra blood will even
make your face reddish. But, then, in a second or so, your
blood pressure falls back down to normal and the extra
blood drains from your face. In this process, your brain gets
a little "oxygen bath," similar to what happens when you
jump rope or play soccer. And of course you move other
muscles in the body when you laugh too, even if you're not
"doubled over" with laughter or "rolling in the aisles."

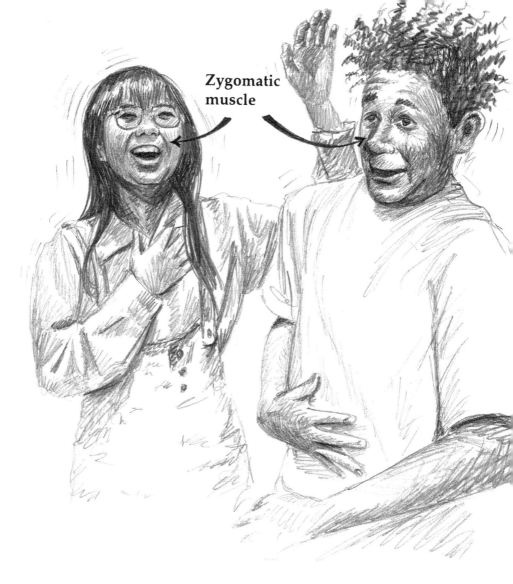

Zygomatic muscle

You laugh for more than a little exercise, though. Laughter seems to relieve tense feelings. It can be major tension, as when you giggle nervously before you go onstage. Or it can be even a very minor tension, as when you see someone make a silly mistake.

Scientists have found that your brain releases antitension chemicals when you laugh. They are called endorphins and enkephalines, natural brain substances that relax you and even cut down on pain. So laugh some more! It's really good for you!

Nail Growing

Your fingernails grow three times faster than your toenails. Toenails grow an inch (2.5 centimeters) about every two years. For fingernails to grow the same length, it takes only eight months. The middle fingernail is the speediest, and the thumb and the little finger grow most slowly. Both fingernails and toenails grow faster in summer and more slowly when you are sick.

A nail is made of dead body cells of a tough substance called keratin. (Your hair is made of another variety of keratin.) The nail is pushed out of the nailbed, hidden under the skin, by living cells there. All this action seems designed just to give you a tool that you can't lose—you use your nails to open things, scratch things, and much more!

Fingernails and toenails look harder than they are. They are really filled with tiny holes that air and liquids can go through. Water, paint, and nail polish can go right through your nails.

Every 24 hours, you produce about a quart (liter) of saliva. And that's not even for big spitters! Saliva is there to help you start to digest your food and to keep your mouth moist enough for talking, singing, whistling, and so on.

The spit comes out of salivary glands in your mouth. Spit is made mostly of water, but it also contains mucus and two chemicals that help turn your food into something your stomach and intestines can absorb better. The slobber also moistens the food so that it can slide down your throat without getting stuck. Also, your taste buds couldn't even taste your food if your spit didn't make it wet.

When you think about a chocolate doughnut, does your mouth water? That just means your brain has sent an order down to your salivary gland to get ready for food—by making saliva 20 times faster than when you aren't ready to eat anything!

Over your whole lifetime, you will make enough spit to fill a large swimming pool!

Salivary glands

Whap! Whooze! You hit your head or feel dizzy—and you may "see stars." These little points of light come not from the heavens but from inside your head.

The tiny "stars" are flashing signals made by nerve cells in your retina, at the back of your eyeball. The light is made by a few of the 100 million or so nerve cells in that part of your eye—by mistake. This fancy error happens when the normal pathway between eye and brain gets shaken up. It's a little like static on a TV set, when you can't see the picture.

Bumping your head or getting dizzy are the two main ways to "see stars." But you can also get them from an electric shock, a high fever, or even the first stages of anesthesia (when you can't feel pain) before an operation in the hospital.

"SEEING STARS"

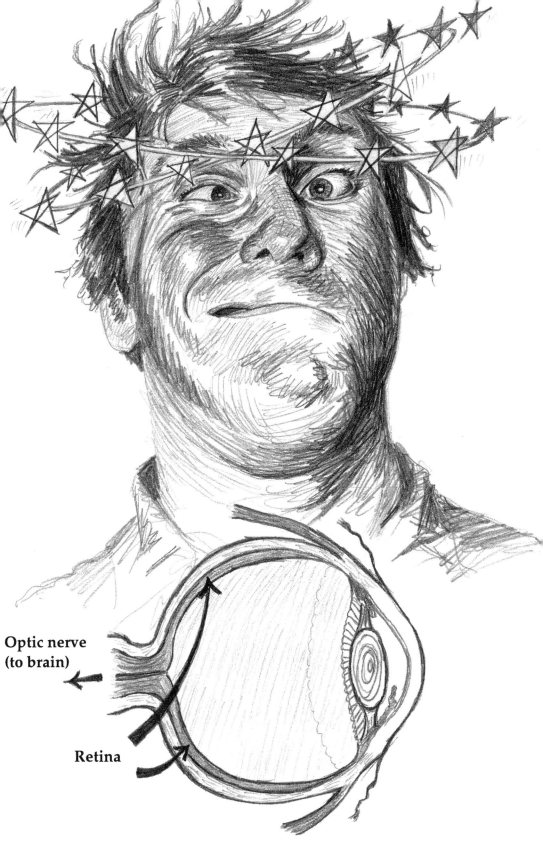

Optic nerve (to brain)

Retina

SHIVERING

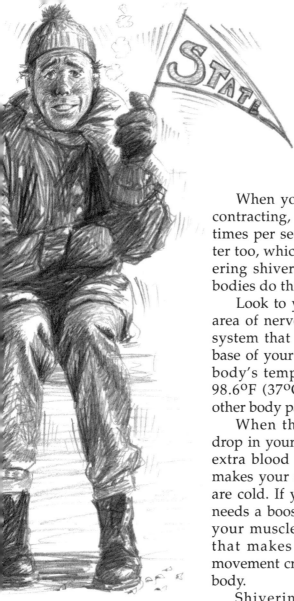

When you shiver, your muscles are contracting, or tightening, as fast as 20 times per second. Your teeth may chatter too, which is just your jaw in a quivering shiver. Why on earth would our bodies do this to us?

Look to your hypothalamus, a small area of nerve cells (part of the nervous system that controls your body) at the base of your brain. Its job is to keep the body's temperature stable, or close to 98.6°F (37°C) inside, so that all your other body parts can work well.

When the hypothalamus senses a drop in your body temperature, it sends extra blood to your skin. That is what makes your skin look redder when you are cold. If your body temperature still needs a boost, the hypothalamus orders your muscles to do the violent twitch that makes you shiver. This muscle movement creates some heat inside your body.

Shivering works well for a little while. But if you stay cold and shiver too long, the muscle action will start to use up too much energy. At that point, your hypothalamus decides that shivering is not good for you anymore. When you're so cold that you stop shivering, you should do something to get warm—and very quickly.

SLEEPING

When you conk out every day for hours on end, there should be some good reason for it! People have pondered sleep for centuries, but scientists still haven't completely decided why we do it.

We do know this: When you sleep, you put "on hold" the most complex organ on earth—the human brain. When you're awake, your brain makes more than 100,000 different chemical reactions every second—and records almost 90 million separate bits of information every day! This is busy!

We are sure of one thing that happens only during sleep. It is the only time your pituitary gland releases a growth hormone, so you grow only when you're asleep. Did sleep come about to allow us time to grow, or were there other reasons?

You are never completely inactive during sleep. You shift positions in bed 40–70 times during an average night, which keeps your blood circulation going. You also go through several

70

stages of sleep, each of which serves different functions for your body. Light sleep, which lasts about 10 minutes, is the first stage. In it your body temperature and blood pressure drop and you breathe lightly. The second stage of sleep—about 20–30 minutes long—comes next, and it is deeper. In this stage, your eyeballs begin to roll behind your eyelids and your brain waves perk up a bit. The third sleep stage is deep relaxation— your temperature and blood pressure are very low. Next comes stage four, REM (rapid eye movement sleep), the time for dreaming.

Throughout the night you go through all these four stages of sleep several times, but the deeper sleep periods and the dreaming periods become longer toward the middle of the night. As you move toward wake-up time, the lighter sleep periods take over. Soon you wake up and get that brain fully alert all over again!

Most adults do not sleepwalk, but about 15 of every 100 kids do! Sleepwalking does not have to mean a half-hour hike through the house. It can even just be sitting up in bed and looking around. In a sleepwalk, you are asleep but your eyes are open, glassy-eyed, for at least a few seconds.

You "sleepwalk" when your brain does not make a perfect change to get you from one sleep stage to another. It can happen especially between deep sleep and dreaming sleep. (For more on sleep stages, see the section on "Sleeping.") If you do sleepwalk a little, you will almost certainly get over it when you get older.

Is it true that no one should wake up a sleepwalker? Yes, usually. Being awakened suddenly could frighten the sleepwalker or cause that person to jump or swat someone. After all, a sleepwalker's judgment is not awake either! But go ahead and wake the sleepwalker if you have to prevent him or her from doing something destructive. At least sleepwalkers don't act out their dreams—for the simple reason that sleepwalking does not happen during the dreaming stage of sleep.

It is best to just guide a sleepwalker gently back to bed. The little hike or staring time will be over soon anyway!

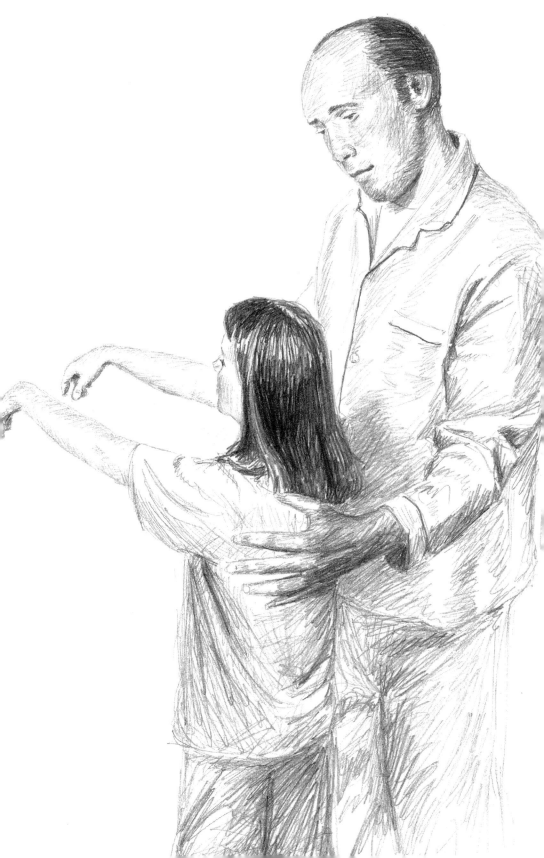

Have you heard that it is easier to smile than to frown? That's true. Smiling is the easiest of the major facial expressions, in terms of what the muscles do.

First, the zygomatic muscle lifts your cheeks up a little. At the same time, it pulls up the corners of your mouth, stretches your lips a bit, and makes the skin below your eyes a little baggy. Also at the same time, the orbicularis oculi muscle makes your eyes narrow a little and the skin around them crinkle. All this adds up to a sincere smile.

A fake smile is a little different. To spot one, look at the person's eyes. Unlike a true smile, a fake one does not usually crinkle the skin around the eyes or flatten them slightly. Scientists even say that these two kinds of smiles are routed through the brain differently.

Many people have wondered where smiles come from. Take a look at the face of a dog or chimpanzee at play first. When the animal is happy, the face drops a little, the mouth lies open in a relaxed way, and the eyes look bright. But when an animal like a chimp has an expression that looks more like your smile—the mouth mostly closed and drawn across the face in a line—it is the sign of a threat or fear.

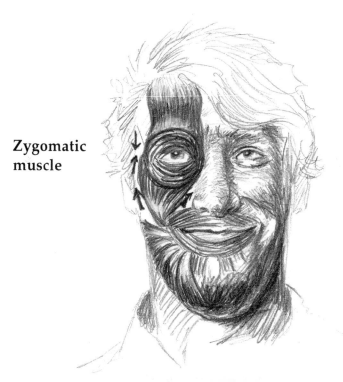

Zygomatic muscle

SMILING

Both of these expressions are probably ancestors of your smiles. A smile may mean you're feeling playful—and it may be what's left after a threat or fear ends in relief. "Whew, that's over," you say—and you smile!

SNEEZING

You sneeze to get rid of something irritating your nose. A sneeze is a very violent breath, blasting out of your nose at 75–100 miles (120–160 kilometers) per hour, faster than the wind in any blizzard! There is usually one of two good reasons for it—a cold or an allergy.

If you sneeze because of a cold, you are actually ah-chooing out tiny virus particles or bacteria. At the beginning and middle of a cold, these little cold-causers are very much alive! So if you sneeze onto people or onto a doorknob or desk that other people touch, they will probably pick up your invisible "gift"—live viruses ready to cause the same cold in them. These viruses can live as long as three hours outside of a human body. Once these people touch their noses, eyes, or mouths by chance, then in go the virus particles, ready for action. They give that person your cold!

If the sneeze comes from an allergy, you fling out chemicals called histamines, along with some of the pollen or dust or whatever irritated your breathing system. The histamine has been made by your body as it tried to fight off the allergic substance. But at least it's not alive!

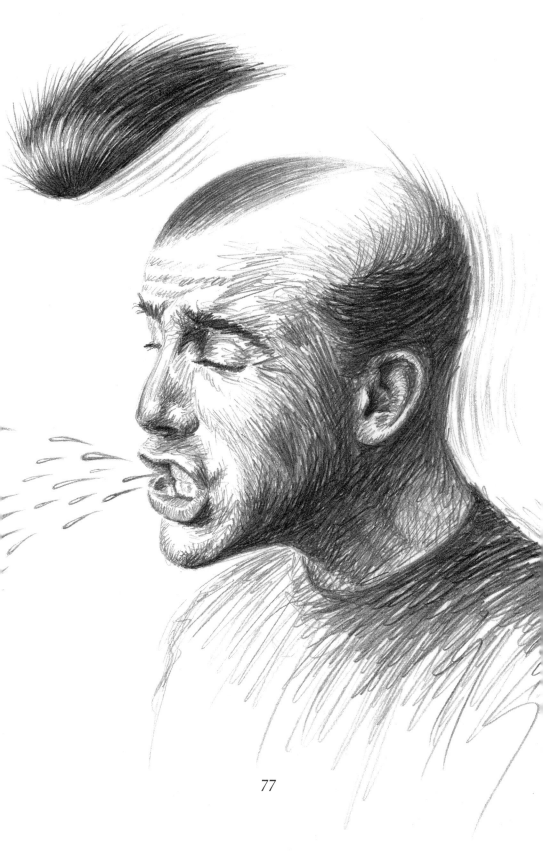

SNORING

It is buzz-saw time! The loudest snore ever measured was 80 decibels–as loud as a jackhammer would sound tearing up the street 10 feet (3 meters) away! Many people snore occasionally, but not usually that loud! You snore because you are not breathing well at night. This can happen when you have a cold or an allergy that affects your breathing. Other causes are enlarged tonsils or adenoids in your throat. Overweight people seem to snore more than thinner ones. In all these situations, the air passageway to your lungs is partly blocked. The lungs then pull in extra air to make up for this. That makes your uvula vibrate. That's the little flap that hangs down the back of your throat. The roof of your mouth even vibrates. The vibration makes the noise of the snore. A few people snore every night! These are often adults who weigh too much, drink too much, eat too much, or have allergies or chronic problems with their tonsils or adenoids. It seems to help for these people to avoid sleeping on their backs. How much do you snore?

SWEATY PALMS AND FEET

Sweating helps keep your body temperature under control. On every square inch of your skin you have an average of 625–650 sweat glands (about 100 per square centimeter), *and* you have about 15 square feet (1.4 square meters) of skin! When the sweat seeps (or pours!) out, it evaporates, which cools you off.

The palms of your hands and the soles of your feet have many more than the average number of sweat glands per square inch (or centimeter). In fact, they have 3,000 per square inch (465 per square centimeter) of skin surface! All these glands are ready to respond not only when you're hot, but when you're ready to go onstage for the solo in the musical or to take a big test! When they let loose, there can be plenty of sweat!

When you feel emotional stress, your body gears up for action. Part of this readiness means you hold heat in your internal organs. Your heart and lungs, for example, can then work harder for you if they need to. But your body also releases heat where you don't need it as much, as in your hands and feet.

Of course it's possible to sweat too much. If you exercise too hard on a very hot day, you will lose so much water that—unless you replace it by drinking—the chemical balance in your body cells will be damaged and you might get very sick! At least this will not happen from nervous stress. But if you sweat a little now and then, it's all right . . . don't sweat it!

Go ahead and try it, but it won't work. You just can't tickle yourself! To see why, you have to think for a moment about why your skin is on you in the first place!

What if a snake were starting to slither across your ankle? Or a tree branch beginning to brush against your face? Or a mosquito swooping down onto your arm? One of the reasons your skin is there is to tell you what's coming at you, what is starting to assault your body from the outside world.

A tickle is automatically understood by your skin as an attack. A small one! The "free nerve endings" (parts of your nervous system that respond to touch) at your skin level send a message to the brain that says, "Something is assaulting us." (These free nerve endings happen to be very densely packed in your armpits, for example.) But then you realize that this is *not* an attack—and you laugh out of relief.

You can't tickle yourself because there is no way that your body can think it's an attack—then laugh—when you're only doing it to yourself.

Tickling Yourself

You tremble, or shake, when you're very afraid, happy, guilty, excited, or even just plain tired! You can even start trembling from eating too much sugar all at once! Your body usually doesn't behave this oddly, but sometimes you do get cramps, twitches, spasms—and trembles.

You shake when your muscles and your motor nerves are briefly out of coordination. The motor nerves are just one group out of our 20 billion nerve cells, all of them under control by our brain and spinal cord—but they are the ones that tell our muscles what to do and how fast to do it. When you tremble from tiredness, blame it more on the muscles. And when you tremble from some sort of emotion, look more to the motor nerves. But they both are always involved in trembling.

When you shake, your muscles contract and relax, contract and relax, over and over again quickly. But then it's finished— and you have nothing to worry about!

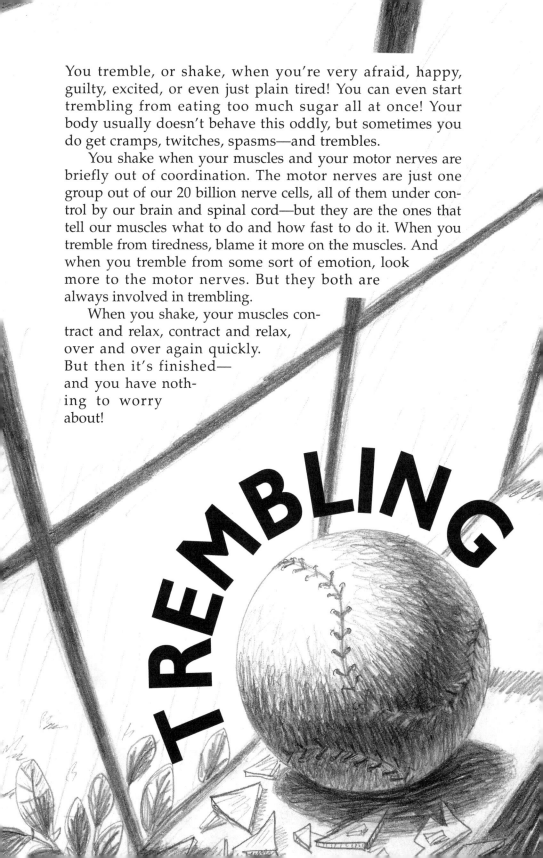

TREMBLING

Vomiting is your stomach's way of coughing! Like coughing, vomiting is the body's natural reaction to something harmful that it needs to get rid of. So vomiting may seem very yucky, but it is actually helping you.

You can vomit from food poisoning, tonsillitis, indigestion, something stuck in your digestive system, various infections (like a stomach "flu"), strong smells, and much more. Even motion sickness and nervousness can sometimes make you vomit—upchuck—throw up.

To make the yucky stuff come up takes powerful muscle action! First your stomach and esophagus (swallowing tube) hold still. Then your diaphragm and abdominal muscles contract. This squeezes your stomach hard. Then you know what happens next!

Luckily, the air passageways in your throat close to keep the vomit out of the lungs. It is dangerous to vomit when you are unconscious because the airways would not close and you could breathe in some of the vomit! Double yuck. But remember, you do need to do it sometimes—so go ahead and barf!

89

When you talk, you exhale air. It comes up out of your lungs, then moves over the vocal cords in your throat, which vibrate in various ways to make the sounds. To shout, you open your mouth and let the sound move through your throat, nose, and even your sinuses—cavities in your head. You push the air up faster and harder too!

To whisper, you don't even move your vocal cords. You just gently hiss the air up through your throat. Psst—can you hear me?

WHISPERING

YAWNING

Try this experiment: Yawn, just once, in a group of friends. Most likely, a couple of them will start yawning too. Then more will. Yawning is, in a way, contagious. (Not like germs are, though!) This is a mystery, still, to scientists.

Some parts of the puzzle are known. Yawning is a reflex, an automatic act to get something in your body back to normal. A little spasm (fast muscle contraction) in your throat muscles throws your mouth open. And when you take the deep breath to make the yawn, you're getting more air into your lungs. You may also be equalizing pressure in your ear. (See the section on "Ear Popping.")

Why would you need extra air in your lungs? Maybe because you were sitting quietly in a warm room, so bored or so tired that you weren't breathing very deeply. You didn't have quite enough oxygen in your blood— and a yawn solves your problem.

GLOSSARY

abdominal (ab-DAHM-in-il) Having to do with your abdomen (AB-duh-min), the part of your body where your stomach is.

anesthesia (an-us-THEE-zhuh) Loss of ability to feel pain, temperature, or even something touching you, as when you're given a medicine—an anesthetic (an-us-THET-ik)—before an operation.

bacteria Tiny living things that can be seen only under a microscope and that live in water, soil, plants, and even your amazing body! Some bacteria help us, and some can make us sick.

blood circulation The movement of blood through your body by the different tubes that carry your blood.

blood clot A group of blood cells that clump together, stopping blood flow in an area.

blood vessels The arteries, veins, and smaller tubes that move blood through your body.

bronchial (BRAHNK-ee-il) **tubes** Tubes between your windpipe and your lungs that help your body breathe in and out.

cell The smallest living unit of your body able to act independently and perform all the functions of life (such as eating, elimination, reproduction).

congest (kun-JEST) To get filled up more than it should (as a nose congested with mucus).

emotions Your feelings.

free nerve endings Parts of your nervous system that respond to touch, such as tickling. In your armpits there are lots of free nerve endings.

glands Groups of cells inside your body that release substances into your blood so your body can work well.

macrophage (MAK-ruh-fayj) A kind of cell within your blood that cleans up injured areas and helps fight infections and other diseases by "swallowing" what it needs to get rid of.

membrane A layer of skin that covers or lines a body part.

motor nerves Parts of your nervous system that control your muscles.

mucus (MYOO-kiss) Thick, slimy liquid that protects sensitive areas such as the inside of your nose.

nervous system In humans, the nerves, the spinal cord, the brain, and all their connections. Your nervous system controls many of your body's reactions to the world.

phlegm (FLEM) A kind of mucus that can build up in your breathing passages.

spasm (SPAZ-im) Sudden, strong contraction of muscles in an area of your body.

virus A living thing, even smaller than bacteria, that causes a disease. Viruses can grow and multiply only inside living cells.

FURTHER READING

Allison, Linda. *Blood and Guts: A Working Guide to Your Own Insides*. Boston: Little, Brown, 1976. Clear overview of human body, plus fun games and experiments—but make sure an adult says they're OK to do and provides supervision.

Aronson, Billy. *They Came From DNA*. New York: Scientific American Books for Young Readers (W. H. Freeman), 1993. Offbeat, funny account of how alien discovers what makes people the way they are. Informative and entertaining.

Day, Trevor. *The Random House Book of 1001 Questions and Answers About the Human Body*. New York: Random House, 1994. Well-organized, easy-to-understand collection of one-sentence questions and one-paragraph answers.

The Eyewitness Visual Dictionary of the Human Body. New York: Dorling Kindersley, 1991. What's what in the human body, clearly photographed and labeled.

Miller, Jonathan. *The Human Body*. New York: Viking Penguin 1983. Not for in-depth information, but enjoy the fabulous pop-ups and pull-tabs.

Parker, Steve. *The Body Atlas: A Pictorial Guide to the Human Body*. New York: Dorling Kindersley, 1993. Oversized, full-color, informative guide to the body one section at a time.

Silver, Donald M., and Wynne, Patricia J. *The Body Book*. New York: Scholastic Professional Books, 1993. Although written for teachers, these "easy-to-make hands-on models that teach" (as the subtitle says) may be the next best thing to constructing your own skeleton. For ambitious learners who enjoy scissors and tape.

Stein, Sara. *The Body Book*. New York: Workman, 1992. Like other books in this series, crammed full of information. Great for browsing.